D1716234

Full **STEAM** Ahead!

Engineering Everywhere

What Does an Engineer Do?

Robin Johnson

CRABTREE
PUBLISHING COMPANY
WWW.CRABTREEBOOKS.COM

Title-Specific Learning Objectives:

Readers will:

- Describe and understand that engineers are people who design things that solve problems and meet needs.
- Identify some technologies that make life easier, safer, and more fun.
- Ask and answer questions about the main ideas of the text, and how engineering solutions work.

High-frequency words (grade one) a, are, did, is, like, made, of, that, the, use, you	Academic vocabulary creative thinking, design, protect, solution, solve, technologies

Before, During, and After Reading Prompts:

Activate Prior Knowledge and Make Predictions:

Have children read the title and look at the cover and title-page images. Ask:

- What do you think this book will be about?
- What is an engineer? In what kinds of places do engineers work?

During Reading:

After reading pages 16 and 17, have children ask and answer questions about the text and pictures. Ask:

- What does it mean to stay safe or be protected?

- Look at the picture on page 16. What technologies protect the boy? How do they protect him?
- Look at the picture on page 17. How do life jackets keep us safe?

After Reading:

Invite children to find an item from home that solves a problem or meets a need. Have each child bring in the item and share it with their peers by presenting it orally. Children should explain whether the item makes life easier, safer, or more fun. They should identify the problem it solves or need it meets.

Author: Robin Johnson

Series Development: Reagan Miller

Editor: Janine Deschenes

Proofreader: Melissa Boyce

STEAM Notes for Educators: Reagan Miller and Janine Deschenes

Guided Reading Leveling: Publishing Solutions Group

Cover, Interior Design, and Prepress: Samara Parent

Photo research: Robin Johnson and Samara Parent

Production coordinator: Katherine Berti

Photographs:
Alamy: NASA: p. 8
iStock: yasinguneysu: p. 4; IPGGutenbergUKLtd: p. 10; FatCamera: p. 17
Shutterstock: MikeDotta: p. 9
All other photographs by Shutterstock

Library and Archives Canada Cataloguing in Publication

Title: What does an engineer do? / Robin Johnson.
Names: Johnson, Robin (Robin R.), author.
Description: Series statement: Full STEAM ahead! | Includes index.
Identifiers: Canadiana (print) 20189061936 |
  Canadiana (ebook) 20189061944 |
  ISBN 9780778762089 (hardcover) |
  ISBN 9780778762676 (softcover) |
  ISBN 9781427122643 (HTML)
Subjects: LCSH: Engineering—Vocational guidance—Juvenile literature.
  | LCSH: Engineers—Juvenile literature.
Classification: LCC TA157 .J645 2019 | DDC j620.0023—dc23

Library of Congress Cataloging-in-Publication Data

Names: Johnson, Robin (Robin R.), author.
Title: What does an engineer do? / Robin Johnson.
Description: New York, New York : Crabtree Publishing Company,
  [2019] | Series: Full STEAM ahead! | Includes index.
Identifiers: LCCN 2018056596 (print) | LCCN 2018059498 (ebook) |
  ISBN 9781427122643 (Electronic) |
  ISBN 9780778762089 (hardcover : alk. paper) |
  ISBN 9780778762676 (pbk. : alk. paper)
Subjects: LCSH: Engineering--Vocational guidance--Juvenile literature.
Classification: LCC TA157 (ebook) | LCC TA157 .J566 2019 (print) |
  DDC 620.0023--dc23
LC record available at https://lccn.loc.gov/2018056596

Printed in the U.S.A./042019/CG20190215

Table of Contents

Crabtree Publishing Company
www.crabtreebooks.com   1-800-387-7650
Copyright © **2019 CRABTREE PUBLISHING COMPANY**. All rights reserved. No part of this publication may be reproduced, stored in a retrieval system or be transmitted in any form or by any means, electronic, mechanical, photocopying, recording, or otherwise, without the prior written permission of Crabtree Publishing Company. In Canada: We acknowledge the financial support of the Government of Canada through the Book Publishing Industry Development Program (BPIDP) for our publishing activities.

Published in Canada
Crabtree Publishing
616 Welland Ave.
St. Catharines, Ontario
L2M 5V6

Published in the United States
Crabtree Publishing
PMB 59051
350 Fifth Avenue, 59th Floor
New York, New York 10118

Published in the United Kingdom
Crabtree Publishing
Maritime House
Basin Road North, Hove
BN41 1WR

Published in Australia
Crabtree Publishing
386 Mt. Alexander Rd.
Ascot Vale (Melbourne)
VIC 3032

Solving Problems

Did you know that children can be problem solvers? You **solve** problems every day. When you solve a problem, you are thinking like an **engineer**!

Jordan's backpack was too heavy to carry after school. He solved the problem by adding wheels to the backpack. Now, it is easy to pull.

Katie cannot fit all of her clothes into her closet. How can she solve the problem?

Emma's ice cream cone fell to the ground. She wonders if there is a way to make sure her ice cream never falls again! Can you help her solve the problem?

Finding Solutions

Engineers are people who design things to solve problems. To design is to make a plan for how something is made or built.

Engineers use math, science, and **creative thinking** to find solutions.

The things engineers design are called technologies.
A technology is something that solves a problem.

A straw and a cup are technologies that help make drinking easier.

A door handle is a technology that helps us open a door.

7

Different Types

There are many types of engineers.
They solve different types of problems.

space suit

Some engineers solve problems in space. They might design space suits. The space suits help humans do jobs in space!

These engineers are designing a tunnel. The tunnel will let a train **travel** underground. A tunnel is a solution when a train cannot travel above ground.

On the Move

Some people cannot walk on their own. Engineers design technologies to help them move from place to place.

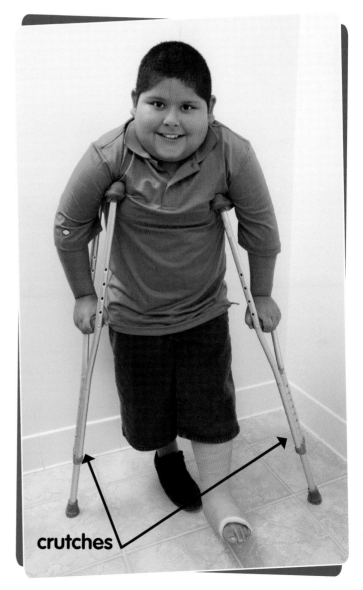

An engineer might design crutches to help people walk.

crutches

wheelchair

An engineer might design a wheelchair to help people move around.

Mighty Machines

Some jobs are hard for people to do. Engineers design machines to solve that problem. Machines are things with many parts. They make work easier.

An engineer might design a **robot** to help build things.

An engineer might design a machine to do work on a farm.

Having Fun

Engineers design technologies that make life more fun. They design new toys and games. They make other toys and games safer to use.

An engineer might design a video game that lets us play with many friends at a time.

Engineers design amusement park rides. They make the rides safer by adding seat belts.

seat belt

An engineer might design a toy that can fly!

Safety First

Engineers keep us safe! They design technologies that **protect** us when we move, work, and play.

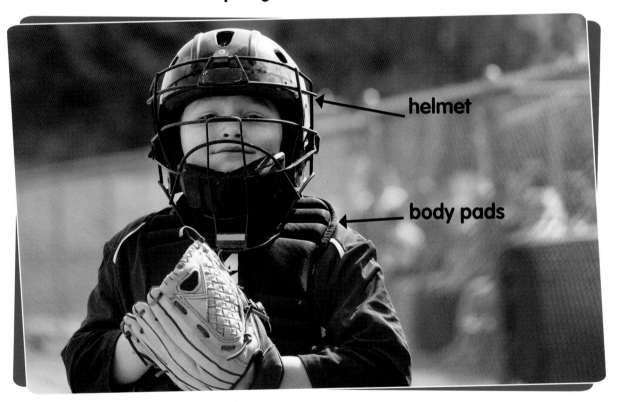

helmet

body pads

Engineers design technologies that keep us safe when we play sports.

life jacket

An engineer might design life jackets to keep us safe near water.

Technology We Wear

Some engineers design technologies that people wear. They can make life easier and safer.

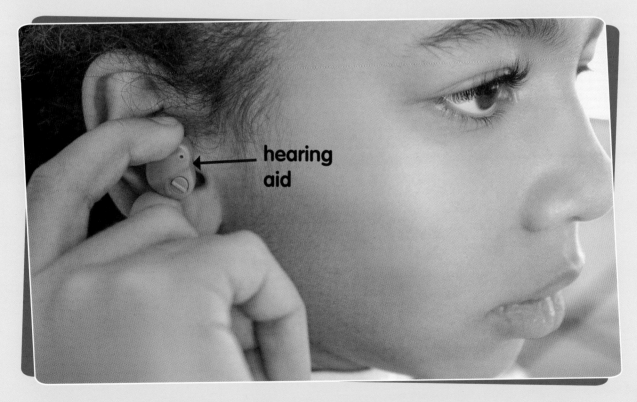

hearing aid

Engineers design hearing **aids**. They help people hear more easily.

An engineer might design gloves that can keep hands warm in very cold weather.

hard hat

An engineer might design a hard hat to keep people safe at work.

Working Together

Engineers work together to find solutions. They think of new solutions. They improve technologies. To improve something is to make it better.

Engineers share what they know and learn from each other.

You can work together with others to solve problems and think like an engineer!

These engineers work together to improve the design of a plane.

Words to Know

aids [eyds] noun Objects or people that help someone do something

creative thinking [kree-EY-tiv THING-king] noun Using your mind to make up new and original ideas

engineer [en-juh-NEER] noun A person who uses science, math, and creative thinking to solve problems

protect [pruh-TEKT] verb To keep from being hurt

robot [ROH-buh t] noun A machine that can do work

solve [solv] verb To find an answer or solution

travel [TRAV-uh l] verb To go from one place to another

A noun is a person, place, or thing.

A verb is an action word that tells you what someone or something does.

An adjective is a word that tells you what something is like.

Index

About the Author

Robin Johnson is a freelance author and editor who has written more than 80 children's books. When she isn't working, Robin builds castles in the sky with her engineer husband and their two best creations—sons Jeremy and Drew.

To explore and learn more, enter the code at the Crabtree Plus website below.

www.crabtreeplus.com/fullsteamahead

Your code is:
fsa20

STEAM Notes for Educators

Full STEAM Ahead is a literacy series that helps readers build vocabulary, fluency, and comprehension while learning about big ideas in STEAM subjects. *What Does an Engineer Do?* uses repeated ideas and categories to help readers answer questions about engineers and the solutions they design. The STEAM activity below helps readers extend the ideas in the book to build their skills in engineering and technology.

My Learning Solution

Children will be able to:
- Use the engineering design process to design a solution that makes learning easier, safer, or more fun.
- Display their solution using technology.

Materials
- Model Planning and Testing Sheet
- Engineering Design Process Worksheet
- Materials for project, including boxes, paper, cardboard, glue, tape, craft sticks, paper rolls, poster board, and art materials
- Chart paper and markers
- *How Engineers Solve Problems* book (optional)
- Digital camera and photo printer

Guiding Prompts
After reading *What Does an Engineer Do?*, ask:
- What does an engineer do?
- Can you think of an example of a solution that makes life easier? Safer? More fun?

Activity Prompts
Explain to children that anyone can think like an engineer! Review the engineering design process. Read the *How Engineers Solve Problems* book (optional). Create an anchor chart that outlines the steps of the process.

Tell children that they will work together in groups to create a solution in their classroom. Their solution must be used by children of their age. It needs to make learning safer, easier, or more fun.

Have a conference with each group to hear their plan. Ensure they have identified whether their learning solution makes life easier, safer, or more fun. When the solution makes sense, have children use the Engineering Design Process Worksheet and the Model Planning and Testing Sheet to plan and test their solution.

When each group has a finished solution, they will use a digital camera to take pictures of their solution in action, showing how it works. Then, children should display the pictures on a poster board. Hold a "display day" in which children showcase their solutions and poster boards.

Extensions
- Have children try the learning solutions for a set period of time and complete a reflective writing activity about how it worked.

To view and download the worksheets, visit **www.crabtreebooks.com/resources/printables** or **www.crabtreeplus.com/fullsteamahead** and enter the code **fsa20**.